illusory borders

heidi reszies

the operating system print//document

illusory borders

ISBN: 978-1-946031-58-7
Library of Congress Control Number: 2019948001
copyright © 2019 by Heidi Reszies
edited and designed by ELÆ [Lynne DeSilva-Johnson]

This text was set in Minion Pro, Taken By Vultures, Freight Neo, and OCR-A Standard.

Books from The Operating System are distributed to the trade by via Ingram, with additional production by Spencer Printing, in Honesdale, PA, in the USA.

The Operating System is a member of the **Radical Open Access Collective**, a community of scholar-led, not-for-profit presses, journals and other open access projects. Now consisting of 40 members, we promote a progressive vision for open publishing in the humanities and social sciences.
Learn more at: http://radicaloa.disruptivemedia.org.uk/about/

Your support makes our publications, platform and programs possible! We <3 You.
Consisder a subscription or sustaining membership today: http://www.theoperatingsystem.org/subscribe-join/

the operating system
www.theoperatingsystem.org

illusory borders

Contents

preface(s) / 9

satellites & margins / 37

Spaces in my living room between objects or spaces between stars are only symbols; blankness is filled with experience.

—Mei-mei Berssenbrugge, *Hello, the Roses*

preface(s)

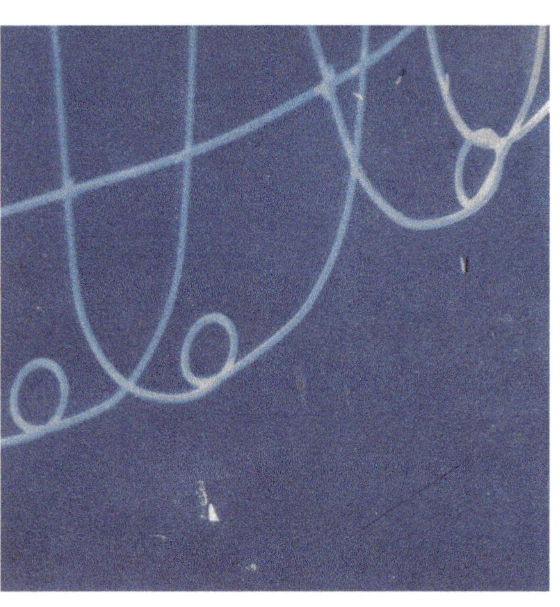

1

This has been designed in mind. Open near a window & grounded.

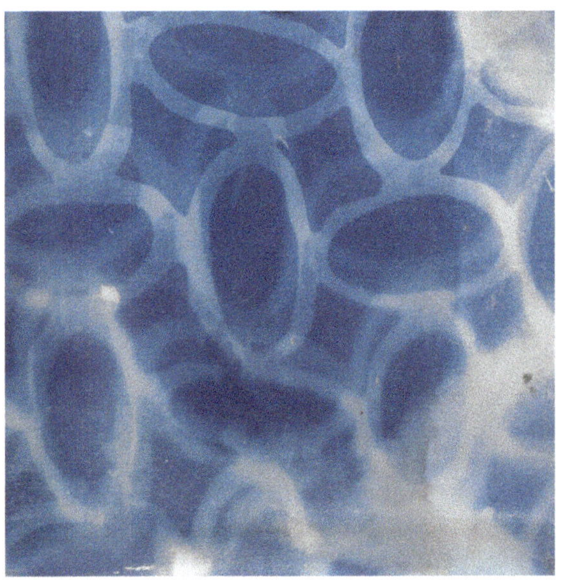

2

The following pages are drawn from material in part/in place/in fact/in light/in gleaning/in verses.

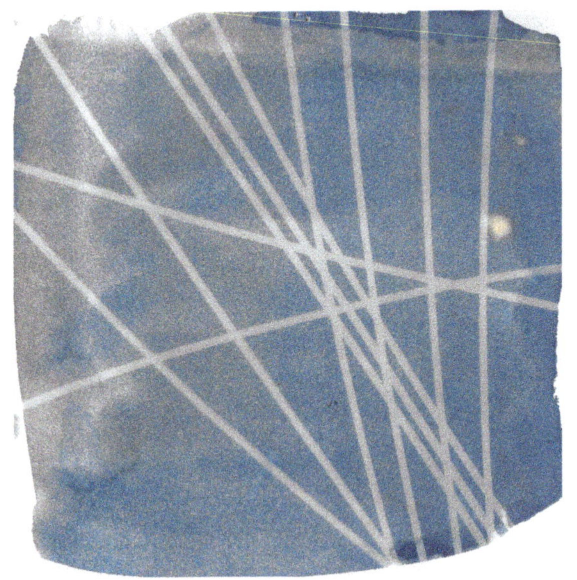

3

You are holding a body scanned & retained as blurred pictures/errant marks. Believe the imperfections/understand the preservation process.

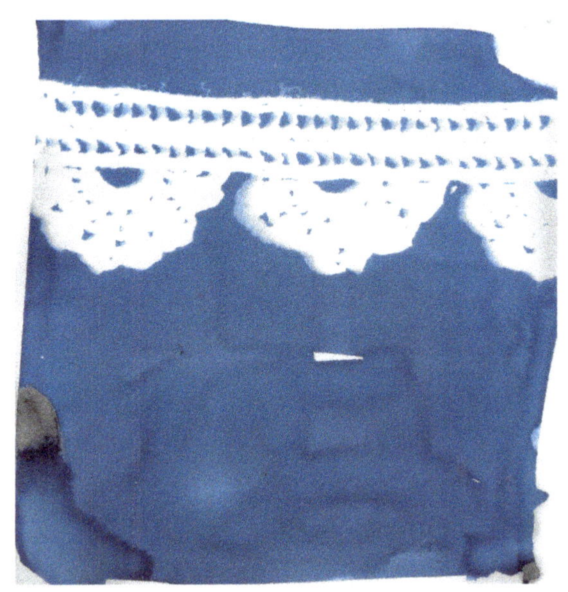

4

Thank you. This was tended as artifacts such as margin notes, errors, missing pages, missing text, &/or always trying to count.

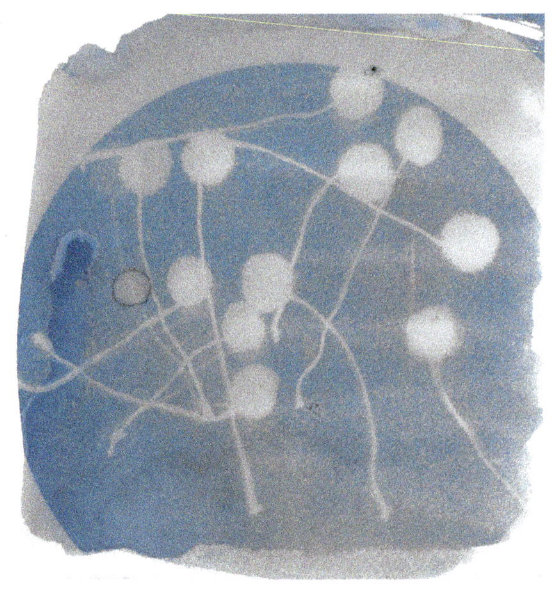

5

I began collecting seeds that day this obscure garden task fulfilled the most complete picture no doubt recognizing hope.

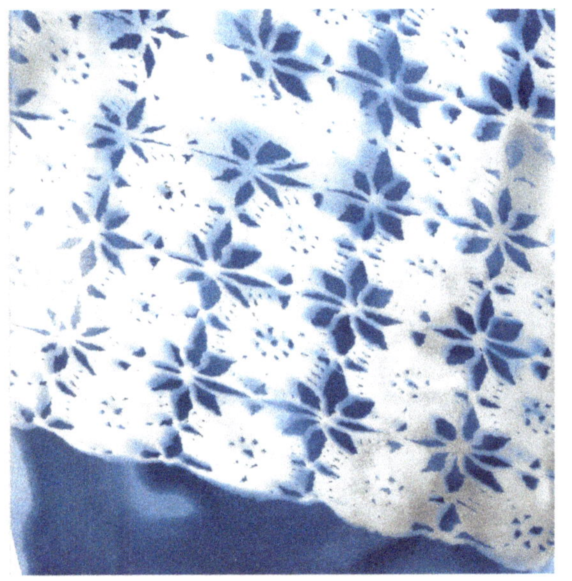

6

The things I was growing in my own garden caught up with me. Even in nature, seeds left questions that flew over time.

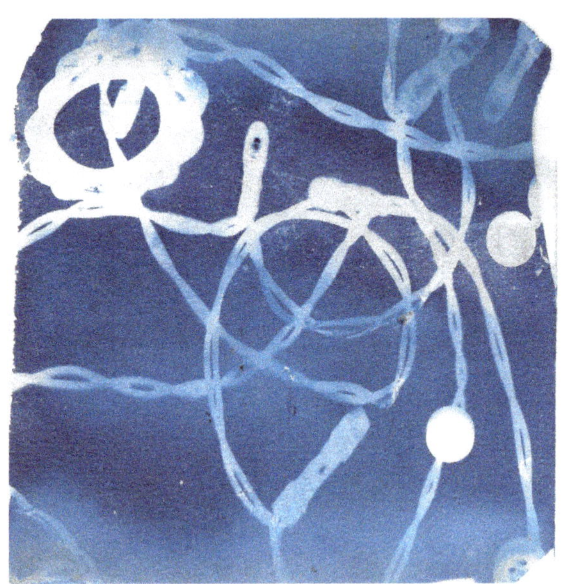

7

I see this translation/propagation borne out of conditions/processes of the mind. An openness emerged from textual & structural aspects. The elucidation/the layers of their present form came from existing configurations/from specific moments in history/in the seem of growth &/or change. Other aspects dealt with purging/ persisting in dire emergencies. The arrangement of certain points/the curve gets lost between the older layers. These do belong/are not independent of the sequence/the page/the first line.

8

in describing/in cultivation/in the strict sense/in the world/in hand/in formation/in time/in September/in December/in nomenclature/in general/in number/in other/in a very small part

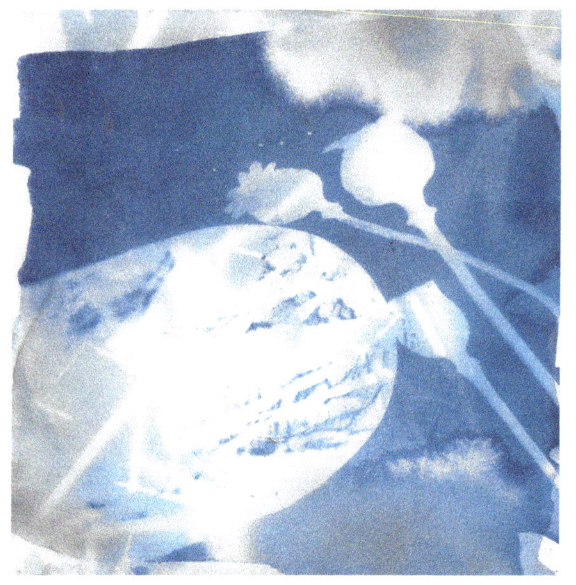

9

I am grateful for every phase of creating. One ignited idea to the next emerged
from my trust.

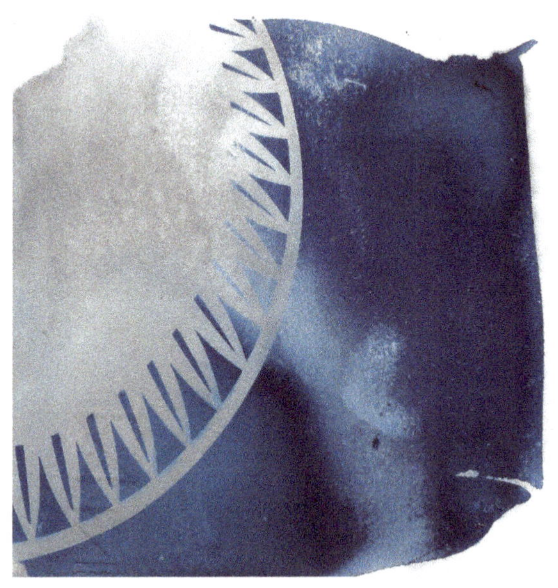

10

Immediacy can capture motion/possibility/a state of paradigms/perspectives of self-organization. The [collection as a] whole can become the field/the sayable. The geometry can be seen as particular dimensionless figures & illustrations. On one hand this can/does happen everywhere & on the other only in black & white images. The text gives the chance to enact the excess of the unsayable.

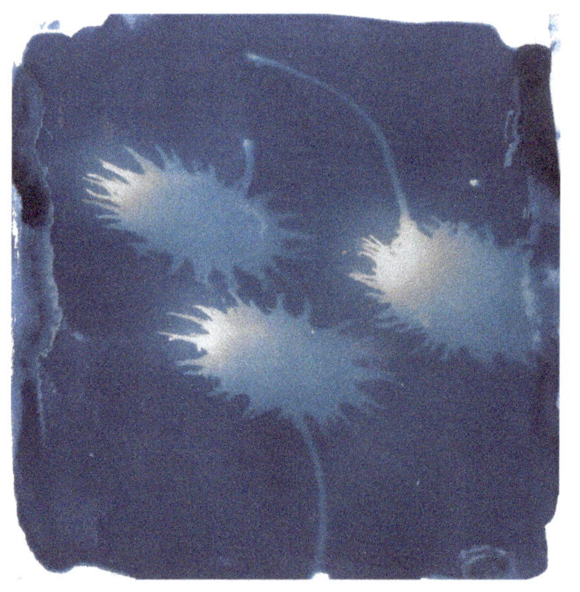

The world/the paper is flat. This rendering displays strategies for enhancing dimensionality in maps/dance movements. Some better than others. It embodies little arrays of typography & color edited & redrawn to make separation/variation/ illustration count. All in all, like mathematics & not tied to space & time.

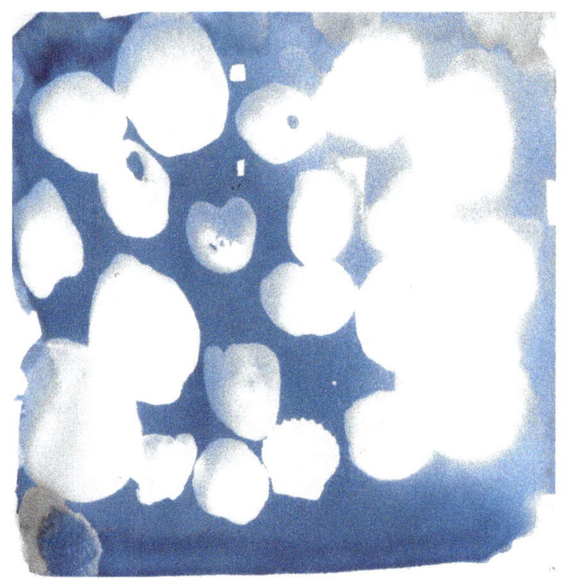

The built-up things keep building. I want to see the whole thing: new things still happening everywhere/every force to reckon with/every little thing. Every body houses doubt sometimes. I think/wonder if I ever really am aware of the motion/ the water/the self. I do not think/I think: that period of vivid intuitions/music everywhere. Everything negatived, everybody quiet for a minute. Yes. Moods in which each thing is very little/all intense. Every time, I worried exactly how to produce it/a cosmos/a portion of the remnant of another thing/everything that has occurred to date/to me.

satellites & margins

This morning
blue seems
absent from
the sky & clouds
are mixing
to make
new hues: puce,
cinereous, some
I don't have
names for.

This morning
blue seems
absent from
the sky & clouds
are mixing
to make
new hues: puce,
cinereous, some
I don't have
names for.

a spectacle

       spreading red
           glittering &

        breakages[1]

---

1   History is this. What it means to be inexhaustible. A force persisting. That spectacle spreading or swinging with an unflagging forward motion. Flood of (un)welcome red. History is this enduring rain that continues without convincing. If history followed the rule of nines, we would grasp how much skin was scorched winging through yesterday's glitter of dragons.

the season   that

                                              is roundness

         wear it

         pink

    a sweet   trimming
    a little

         sewing[2]

---

2   The garden is constantly moving in circles. Late July is fat with yellow pin cushion sunflowers. There are melons swelling on their vines & the heavenly blue morning glories aren't trying to be beautiful. Still they attract the most emphatic pollinators. Just once I want to dress entirely in giant zinnias. Wear the ones in shades of vermilion under my skirt. Pink around the border.

wishing

supposing
there was

scatter-

        ing   one way[3]

---

3   Sometimes I confuse forgiveness with forgetting. I'm driving & at each red light I ball up into fetal pose (not splayed) at the intersection where pavement is a yielding cushion. None of this was a dream. Everything hits at once.

the thing

heaviness

in the morning   that

fainting[4]

____

4   Where once I would have said it's nothing, this morning it's like spring. When the ground gives, it alters everything. Where I was once tilting, now I've unhinged. Close to the epicenter there are ways that fainting can be avoided. They say aftershocks decrease with time. This is how scientists would size me up: unpredictable with the potential to collapse buildings.

making

melody
        not empty
space[5]

---

5   In the picture frame, negative space does not equal absence of ground. The silence between the notes makes music. Our eyes require a place to rest, winding down each line that light carves along the curves of a chair. When I'm seated, see how that chair becomes an extension of me. As the subject, the chair could stand alone. But together we become a marriage of slopes & angles. An appealing composition if we achieve balance.

a

single rose

in earnest   in-

side[6]

---

6   Summer has thinned to one rose still blooming. Nasturtiums escaping borders. Fall wants to muffle what's left of the bees' hum, bearing down on the hive's winter cluster: where they cling together, shivering. It's remarkable how they hold on. The whole crush.

a climb   a

desperate

                    clock   this

                              feeling[7]

____

7   I recall feeling light. The best part of the flight was just before we climbed
into the down. Before the clouds closed in on me. From this distance I could still see
the trees & flailing arms waving goodbye or come home. Before I knew which arms
would get in the way, the way arms can when you're holding your love lying beside
you. Flying, I remembered falling & hours that were all arms. What makes us link falling
with love? Why not folding? For the sake of illustration, tear a page out of a book &
say this is your body. Fold it by halves, over & over again. Continue this sequence of
temporal folding until your body is small enough to smuggle into a foreign country. I
heard someone say the past is a foreign country. Who was I lying flat?

When light
reaches it
all color is
movement so
no single hue
can be viewed
on its own
dancing as if

life depends

        on it.

When light
reaches it
all color is
movement so
no single hue
can be viewed
on its own
dancing as it

life depends

on it.

a box   sometimes

see to the holes
use   paper

the one

being

the other[8]

---

8   This memory: the box of ashes labeled temporary container. Everything moves
from one uncertainty to another. Even after death. By principle, see it through. See to
the holes. Why not box up all we have now & bury it in the garden? Notice how even when
planted upside down, a bulb will by nature turn toward light & right itself. There's a name
for this persistence. Couldn't we invert everything that's familiar, just to see what breaks
through? What opens up. Sometimes blooms are borne on the slimmest stems.

the arrangement

corners   left open in
                    summer

                        & winter

                            winged

that white
that is to say

an increase

                    more than

                        ever[9]

---

9   Standing in front of the full-length bedroom mirror I practiced looking necessary & noticed that once I leaned far enough into my reflection, the picture frame expanded to reveal an open corner with strange evening light around objects. Windows impinging on white walls of a wing I might have inhabited in an inverse life. A view more complete than the sum of its parts: this must be what a bird sees just seconds before it hits the glass.

washing

the same thing

a string   a kind of

nothing
particular

that one
        that

shows[10]

---

10   I am tugging sleeves right side out. I am separating delicates from whatever else. Bleaching whites whiter still & still romancing the idea of liquid bluing. I am screening what is caught in the lint trap & finding the contents of each pocket's deepest pockets. All of this in no particular order. Threads ripped from strung-out seams. Knotted-up gut strings. Remnants of silk lining. What cycled through another week's sulky tangle. Always something needing mending.

neglect

                        a certain

            supposing

    suppose

    the rest[11]

/// 52 ///

11   On my desk, the disarray is slipping like plates. Tectonicus: from the Greek, pertaining to building. How layers meet & move is all up to the moon. Its tidal forces. What falls between precedent & precipice in the dictionary—what can be built to span that hollow? Suppose I just leave chasms to cleave open. Prune the roses.

this state   of

present   the

occasional dark[12]

---

12   I woke up aware of everything housed in my ribcage quaking & my limbs. I woke up aware of my eyes weighed down by the ceiling. How removed I'd become from objects. This is what happens when I fake nothing happening, I think. What happens to all the furniture & the walls of this room under a blanket of darkness: they disappear. When the moon disappears, I'm aware of its constant floating in space or occasional ballooning within the walls inside me. I woke up aware of this balloon & a gust of wind suggesting somewhere a winter storm had already begun. Here in the present, the ceiling is just beginning to fall. Snow gathers with a sense of ritual. The garden still asleep in this lightening. An upswing of bare branches.

the

current   a   blue   line[13]

---

13   Silence falls in drifts. This sound is repeated until the garden reveals nothing: a deep canvas of snow growing more luminous by the hour. When I hold a blank page up to a window, note the illusory blue border. The thin line between moving & moving away. How dark the relative constancy of white paper flatland appears in this context. Whether read horizontally or vertically. Even tilted toward the light, all brightness lies beyond it. I've forced light indoors in the form of twigs flowering lemon yellow on the kitchen table. Also in between mirrors, so the effect multiplies indefinitely like wallpaper.

                another   blue

        particular

        all   the waving
                                      color

        scarcely   standing[14]

---

14   My blue shadow searching for stillness drifts instinctively to windows: their panes,
separate golden sections. How clouds have worked themselves through to interiors. All
the cotton wound up in knots. At the window, I'm flying again. This time, over waving
color & an ocean tonguing the map's feathered edges to some far-off archipelago. Maybe
because I've read how certain birds settled on isolated islands. How without the threat
of predators, they traded flight for more grounded forms of locomotion. Even birds
acknowledge the extreme demands of flying.

shadows
blooming

hope

&   nothing

less[15]

<hr>

15   Some days I only speak in pictures. As in my impressions of shadows looming where flowers once bloomed. Or reflections on surfaces until every surface becomes a mirror. Picture the nature of this cloudiness as it appears through the window: grey situated somewhere between extremes, as in a black & white photograph. In the window grey is illuminated—a little aspiration depicted as a hint of color. Today grey surfaces in blue tones. The walls of this room should be painted this hue: weakly luminous against objects. Where object implies body, a sort of darkening. A part of me turned toward the window & part of me away.

bending

more than necessary

not more   than

that[16]

____

16   Every time I attend to a seedling bending more & more toward the sun, I accept
that this planet is round. Doubting only occurs after believing. I believe I have never been
to the moon & back again.

the missing   (not the

                              misplaced)

the lesson that is

            nothing   just so much

                                          making[17]

____

17   There are words left. I'm winnowing words & caching them away, pressed along
the seams or against the roof of my mouth. Phrases tuck securely behind my knees while I
sleep. My pockets are stockpiles. I'm making layers of nacre lining & odes to dandle down
the hollows of my bones, where they mingle with marrow.

a well-placed

                              center

a blind

more   mending

                    a whole[18]

---

18   I'm here & I'm also here framed by a window. It's January outside. Inside so many
months have been swept under the rug. It's complicating our furniture arrangement.
I've painted all the walls white so they recede into drifts. Now I'm at an opening waiting
for snow. O Vermont, how I loved your heavy blanket. Here I can't ignore the exhausted
furrows in the garden & the depression forming where I buried our dog that September.
This view makes me want to rake every bed with my fingers & strip each limb bare until I
rip open. Doesn't everything ripen in summer? What keeps me returning to the beginning.
What keeps me asking: if the garden stands for each loss there ever was, what is the
ocean? I want to sail a boat that is not a bed in my dreams.

cloth

several

oceans

why wander
when
wondering is

plenty[19]

---

19   Home is a building. Walls around a center within the hold. Holding place where harmonious arrangements are established. Belongings in drawers where they belong. Cloth & clothing in white & several oceans of color. Needle & thread for those occasions that require mending. There are instances when the scissors wander from drawer to drawer. When we can't find the scissors, we move in circles. The chairs move with us. When we dance we move the kitchen table. We wonder if we've collected enough boxes to hold our belongings. When a home is empty all you have is an empty box. A temporary container.

a paper   likeness

the
          sudden
          between

the

spoon wound   sympathetic
                              strings[20]

---

20   While you slept, my likeness was slip-streaming over astonishing meadow, resembling a paper cutout or soft wool caught in the qualm somewhere in that bitter lingering between flying & swimming. When the silver sliver of moon punctured the surface, perhaps you caught a glimpse of the house I keep inside. The fabric that strings across a cadence of windows. Extra strings repeated in the closed curves of my rib cage. What I fold into my hope chest.

sullenness   a

simple

separation[21]

---

21   Because you couldn't see how color was the difference between an object & its movement, you could be satisfied with static red tulips & completely miss the sway of saturated cups brimming with alizarin crimson. At one particular moment they were madder lake—meaning deeper than a wound inside of a wound—where the petals overlapped. A little less so where they had begun to separate & sweep outward at the lip.

a

little

collapse

in

between[22]

---

22   When summer left, I fell asleep saving a space in the bed. Now even wool won't warm that widening absence. Rain falls in sheets flooding every porous surface. A river swells week by week on the brink of its margins. It's pouring out. I'm pouring out. It only hurts when I breathe. It only hurts when I breathe & open my eyes or blink, so I lie in corpse pose & practice a kind of collapsing: falling deeper & deeper behind my eyes to see where the mind will travel. Along the curvature of Earth. As I fall toward it, its surface curves away.

in

between &

perfectly

unprecedented

satin[23]

---

23   Remember how we stopped to marvel at the picture windows on West 12th Street. At sundown they were lit like silver screens as if the stars meant to draw us in to their satin geometry & hold us there. If not to watch them watching television, to ponder this unprecedented splice between the vernacular, or awe us with their sheer exposure.

                    A flood of
                   blue can fold
                backward on itself
                  through a tiny
                      window or
               arrow into a lung
               so I split open to
              water & sky, mostly
                    to change.

A flood of
blue can fold
backward on itself
through a tiny
window or
arrow into a lung
so I split open to
water & sky, mostly
to change.

necessary

blank spaces

                        the least

              little

                                light[24]

____

24   A margin is the blank space that envelops the content of a page or a window. Where I often cling, bordering on the edge of a foreign country. Did you notice the margins between & under the furniture? I cleared them just so we could see the ocean floor again. A little light helps to separate one object from another. Makes the text more legible.

leaning
                volumes

                                        more change
                                        pressing

        what watermelon there is &   moon

        & moon   widening   more[25]

____

25   My sorrow can feather seamlessly between pages or press against leaning
volumes. It can fold into creases of maps. Slip under my eyelids. Sometimes my sorrow is
so small, no one notices when it drinks water thundered down with gin. Driving home, my
sorrow wants to take the wheel. Today I stopped to let a young father cross the street with
his four small children. He smiled at me, happy I'd waited even after the light went green &
I wondered if his sorrow was something his wife carried for him. Sometimes I carry other
people's sorrow, too. Like the woman at the market pushing her shopping cart with one
watermelon. My sorrow is there in the line where I remember my high school geometry.
Between two points there is always another. A line never extending to a point without
reaching beyond it: this is called a ray. So let's say my sorrow is always half-way there, or
already raying beyond this point to the next one.

all bolts &   this   that table

looking necessary[26]

---

26   After all the lightning & rain sheeting down, what remains is everything that is insoluble: questions about being & becoming. At the window between a cloud & another cloud, I pinned my gaze on a hummingbird whose sole purpose was to dive for blue salvia & tongue deep into each quivering calyx. This is natural when a bird is continuously just hours away from the point of starvation & the flowers are flaunting their saturation with no notion of apologizing for their invasiveness. Why I cut all their petals out of the picture with my sharpest scissors & positioned that table away from the window, back to the negative space at the center of the kitchen. Where more than once, I unraveled over the lettuce. In this light, the edges appear much less startling. As if the table always belonged there & was indispensable.

a   little
collapse in   between[27]

---

27   Home is a still-life arranged on the kitchen table: these tangerines I chose for
you for their vermilion. As if they're saying I can't contain my happiness & this must be
the place, drawing attention away from details that slipped through cracks like the dirge
accumulating in this separation of tongue & groove in our floorboards.

a

hollow   a

chosen

            point[28]

---

28   I'm leaning toward this window: an opening that frames a pane. A thin skin of ice
built up while we were sleeping. Now morning illuminates this intricate crystalline filter. A
veil. Like the leaded glass window of a church we sometimes attend, just show up. While
I'm attending this one aspect of November, my exhalation clears a spot on the glazing: a
window inside another window inside. How many metaphors fit? I zero in on the steel blue
luster of that starling, then drift to the cluster of dried drupelets still clinging to the tip of
a branch. What about the seeds inside them—how hard does the flesh cling?

a grey sky

& nearly

that   dark[29]

---

29   Hinging on December, the door opens to somnolent beds & borders. Dormant euphorbia & patches of void where the zinnias flourished all summer. Now cardinals have nowhere to hide, darting from limb to limb between darknesses. Meanwhile I try to close the distance growing between myself & that vanishing point: all the color I can recall arranged in a vase on the kitchen table. Today grey clouds the most lasting impression. Even paintings on the walls have nearly disappeared.

so

much

grey[30]

---

30   It's February & our heavy coats have been apologizing for our bodies all winter.
I'm sorry I dressed in the same grey sweater for four weeks straight, but it was cashmere
& vaguely unobtrusive. I'm sorry for behaving like a wallflower. I'm sorry I was barely aware
of the dogwood limbs branching out along the periphery. Now their grey is brushing up
against the foreground, obscuring my first person account: that rupture between what I'm
imagining & what I think I'm imagining. I think they've been wearing the same self-effacing
buds all winter. I imagine them bursting open.

a little col-

lapse in

between[31]

---

31   I try drawing in more light to fill the gaps. Like smiling at people in line at the post office stockpiling Forever postage. This makes me question if forever can be measured with any degree of accuracy. I've glued forever to an envelope & wondered if anyone else was grappling with this notion of permanence & attachment. Is it obvious I'm drifting? I've lost count of days I couldn't bear to look at the Love stamp display because it reminded me how some of us love with such abandon. Like continents colliding.

a
little

collapse   in between[32]

---

32   In the garden, rules of punctuation are constantly evolving. A month ago I could see my breath. Now furrows mark clauses & there are paths to disambiguate beds. For emphasis, a mound of thyme where I buried a hummingbird. Daffodils blooming between ellipses. A clump of comfrey to hold attention: the kind of silence that grows between one thought & another. Pea shoot, a single green virgule pause preceding this garden bench full stop. Where I notice poppies sprouting parenthetically & remember how last summer was accented in asterisks. Their millions scattered with no obligation to grow.

a little

collapse in   between[33]

---

33   Because repetition is a form of change, I draw the curtains every morning in every room. Beginning again & again is second nature. Like spring greening. Seedlings pushing through the surface despite the planet's gravity pulling back. I'm pressed against a window expecting daybreak: yes, today will be different.

little

this means

more[34]

---

34   I remember April for its contradictions. Bare limbs & wearing her best dress. Sowing & unearthing. Facts & fantasies. The garden advancing in little increments & buds shooting forth. I remember digging shallow & deep, forgetting the curve I'd come from or where I wanted to be planted. Full sun or shade. Their interstices widening, then hemming in. Nothing & everything else. I remember saying a bed is never just a bed, neither here nor there.

needless

next
best[35]

---

35   At this moment this seedling is my excuse for forgetting every other spring. What is worth remembering when there is real work to do? My diaries are mostly blank books. I don't throw those months away. In context they act as intervals between breaths. Suspended states of being full or empty. I remember feeling abstract. That continuum could only be limned in thin blue horizons.

little piece   of

hope

that joins

flowers
& sky[36]

---

36   Build backward to the beginning. This time to when the rain softened everything. When morning was that porous border we pressed our skin against. We were born as verbs not nouns, infinitives pulled by everything that pulled everything that pulled. The moon: it's still there. A seam of light under a shut door. Outside, flowers inclined to go to seed so optimistically: a sign that we have a garden to fall back on.

a

lip   a

point[37]

---

37   There is this tendency to linger at edges. These places feel familiar. Along a window ledge. Where buildings meet sky & river banks. Trimmed in gold luster, a porcelain cup rim. Paper margin & scissor. Notched collar stitching. Picot & fringe & fray. How petals frill at the lip. A vermilion border. My last dream before waking.

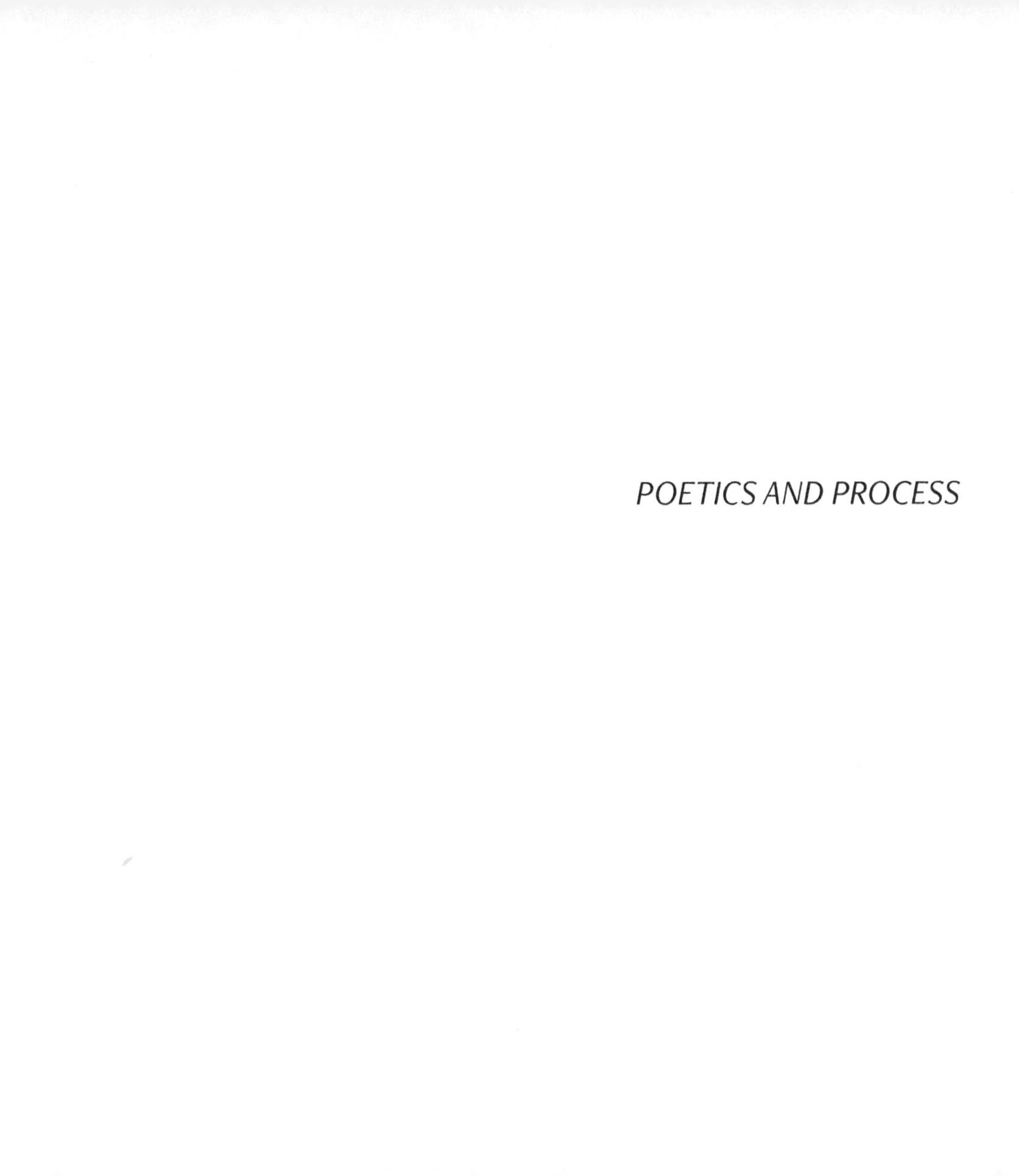

POETICS AND PROCESS

ACKNOWLEDGMENTS

Many thanks to the editors of *Forklift Ohio, FORTH Magazine, BOAAT Journal, Leveler, La Vague Journal,* and *Salt Hill* for publishing earlier versions of poems from this collection.

All my gratitude to ELÆ [Lynne DeSilva-Johnson] for their vision and care in releasing this book into the universe, and to everyone at The Operating System for their generous support.

ABOUT THE AUTHOR/ARTIST:

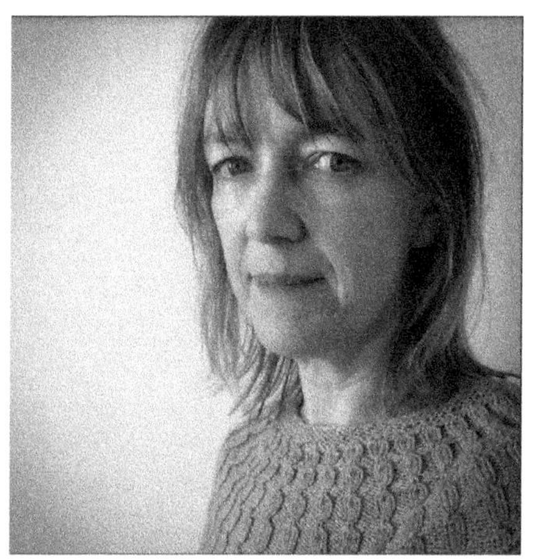

HEIDI RESZIES is a poet and transdisciplinary artist. She earned an MFA in Writing with a concentration in poetry from Vermont College of Fine Arts, and was a 2015 James Merrill Poetry Fellow at the Vermont Studio Center. Her poetry collection titled *Of Water & Other Soft Constructions* was selected by Samiya Bashir as the winner of the Anhinga Press 2018 Robert Dana Prize for Poetry. She is the founding creator/curator of Artifact Press, and currently resides in Richmond, Virginia where she teaches letterpress printing at the Virginia Commonwealth University School of the Arts. Find her at heidireszies.com.

The images that appear on facing pages in 'preface(s)' are original cyanotype prints of Reszies', each measuring 8 x 8 inches, from the series/work in process titled *Blue-ing*, from 2015.

My first poetry collection, *Illusory Borders*, is forthcoming from the OS in 2019. This manuscript was written over the course of about a year and a half—from 2014 to 2015. Since then it has lived under different titles, and the formatting of the text has evolved. In preparation for publication, I've been revisiting/rediscovering my notes, journals, early drafts, correspondence, and various ephemeral materials collected throughout this process of vision and revision—many of which I hadn't seen since they'd been boxed up when I relocated to Richmond, Virginia in August of 2015.

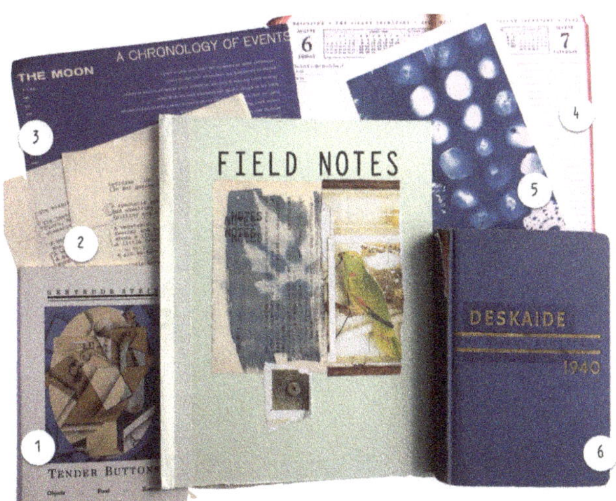

Illusory Borders is grounded in a process that incorporates fragments, lists, and reflections on 'woman's work.' I typically describe it as being inspired, in part, by my reading/rereading of Gertrude Stein's *Tender Buttons*—in particular, the section titled 'Objects'; in retrospect, this poetic series involved more of a confluence of galaxies, with Stein's text situated at one of several significant points of convergence. The images here illustrate (some of) my inspiration throughout the process, the overlap of ideas and sources that fueled the work.

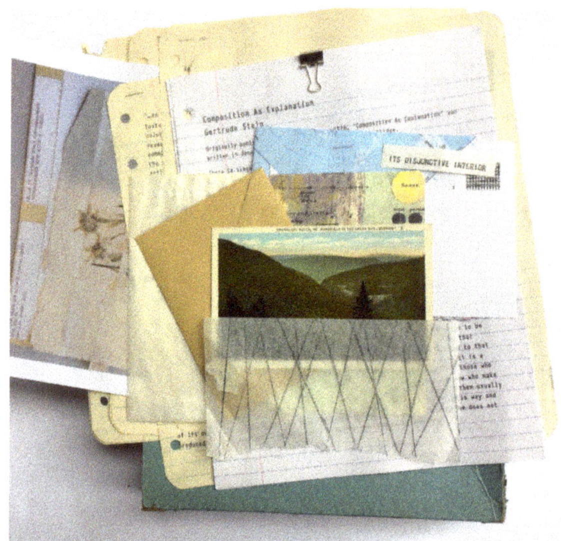

Stein's 'Objects' reminded me of something I'd filed away years before because I knew it would come in handy some day: a 1943 daily planner called a DESKAIDE Silent Secretary. "The Deskaide comes to aid you—as a second mind; to multiply your memory; an efficient, never- failing secretary in well arranged book form, " the book's introduction claims. Only a few pages were written on in this particular planner/diary. Entries like, "Burned by exploding can of butterbeans—I did not go to the doctor on this date," or "Mother's Day—I sent Mother hose and cakes," made an impression.

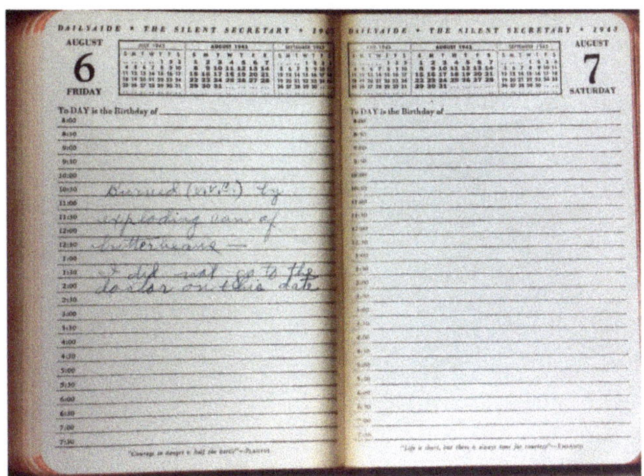

Stein's text and the Deskaide artifact together inspired a list poem, with the working title Tend to. This was composed of fragments of language that I'd scissored out of Objects and collaged in an arrangement/chronology of events that mimicked a cyclical calendar. The title itself was an erasure: T e n d e r B u t t o n s.

Lists naturally for a while and by lists I mean a series.
-Gertrude Stein, from *Composition as Explanation*

My list poem was something I explored/enacted in different ways over time. One of the most important discoveries I made during this process was that writing poems in series/sequence is natural for me. In my twenty-five years of practice as a visual artist (before I came to poetry) I had always created paintings (or prints or collages or assemblages, etc.) in series. Up until this point, the way I'd been writing poems felt by contrast disconnected, but once I allowed those two parts of my creative self to merge—artist and poet—the work that emerged felt like a true extension of me.

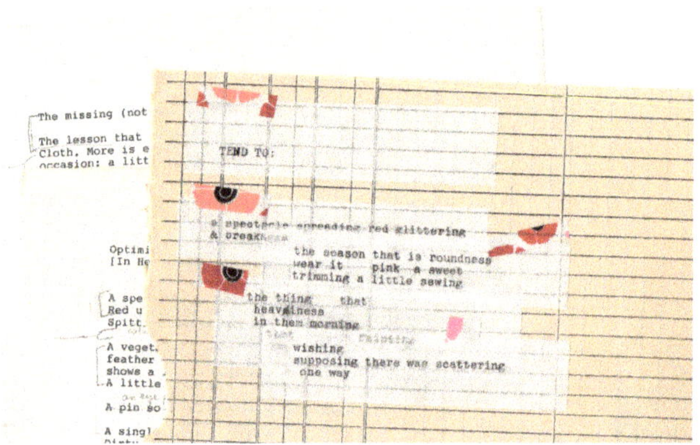

Beginning again and again, writing in manageable units and whenever I had the chance/the energy, writing through and into rupture...eventually I had a text/textile stitched together with fragments that I'd cut and collaged from my original list. This resulting series/long poem seeks to expand liminal spaces, marginality, the unsaid— the footnotes of dailyness and everyday objects.

pictured in FIELD NOTES diagram: 1/ *Tender Buttons*, Gertrude Stein 2/ my list poem, Tend to, in process—typed on a manual typewriter, with handwritten notes 3/ *The Moon—A Chronology of Events* (page from a antique picture book about the solar system 4/ sample spread from a 1943 DESKAIDE 5/ one of my cyanotype prints from a year-long series 6/ 1940 DESKAIDE Silent Secretary (my own journal/notebook)

About six months or so into writing the poems that became the body of work now titled *Illusory Borders*, I began experimenting with cyanotype prints. As I'm typing this *Field Note*, I recall my inspiration, something I'd forgotten until now. While preparing to paint the walls of my son's bedroom (moving objects/clearing space) I came across his high school photography portfolio, which included a few examples of camera-less photography—photograms in particular, which are made by placing objects on a photosensitive surface and exposing them to light. One of these was a cyanotype print—more commonly known as a blue print or sun print—on a sheet of paper that was obviously commercially-produced (the type you can purchase in a kit from a craft store or online). I'd had some experience, years before, applying liquid photo-emulsion to paper for pinhole photographs, and decided to research the chemistry and process involved in cyanotype printing.

That which takes us by surprise—moments of happiness— that is inspiration.—Agnes Martin

I remember what I can only describe now as a feeling of profound joy as I began my blue experiments. As the process unfolded, each step felt new and familiar at the same time, in a sort of bodily knowing.

Like an alchemist, I began by mixing chemicals, some that required heating or crushing with a mortar and pestle. Then, with a soft-bristled brush, I applied a thin wash of emulsion (equal parts of potassium ferricyanide and ferric ammonium citrate solutions, with a bit of citric acid) onto sheets of paper (vellum surface Strathmore bristol and Fabriano Rosaspina printmaking paper)—all of this after dark, in a spare bedroom, where I could leave the paper to dry under the bed until morning.

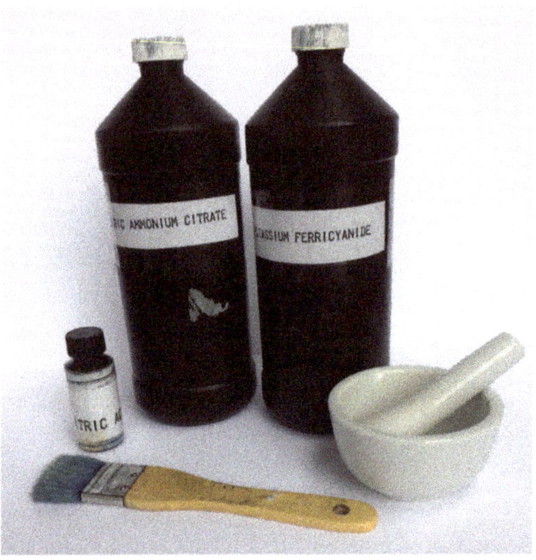

My first test print was on a postcard-size piece of paper, which I tucked under my shirt in order to block the sunlight while I quickly gathered a few sprigs of parsley in the garden (leaves and flower/seed heads), then set paper with my plant material arranged on top in a sunny spot for several minutes. After the appropriate exposure time, I brought the paper indoors to be rinsed in the kitchen sink; what resulted was the white silhouette of parsley against the most intense Prussian blue. I dove deep into this hue and was reminded of a song lyric—from Björk's *The Anchor Song*— *I dive into it / down to the bottom / underneath the currents / and drop my anchor / this is where I'm staying / this is my home.*

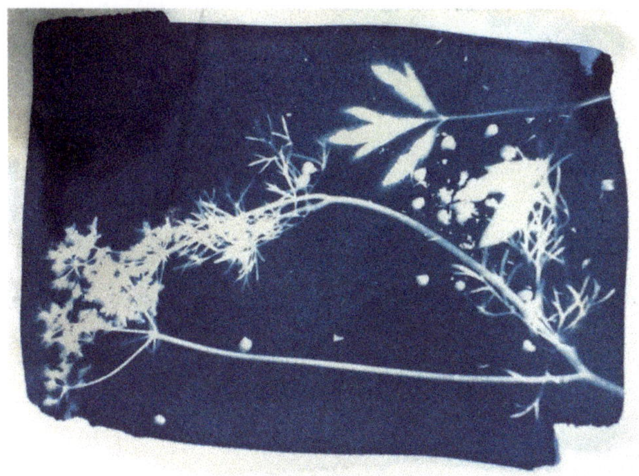

My test print was just the beginning. Soon I had incorporated an almost daily practice of creating cyanotypes—a ritual of painting, drying, arranging, washing, drying...On sunny days, when I was not making poems, I was writing with light (*photo-graph*)— my *poiesis* took the form of blue impressions.

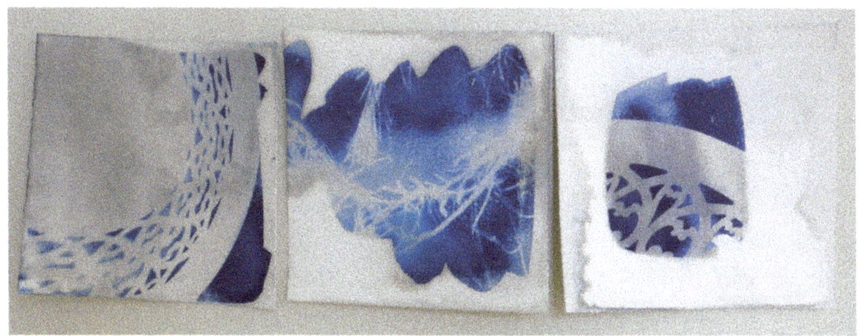

Moon & Moon

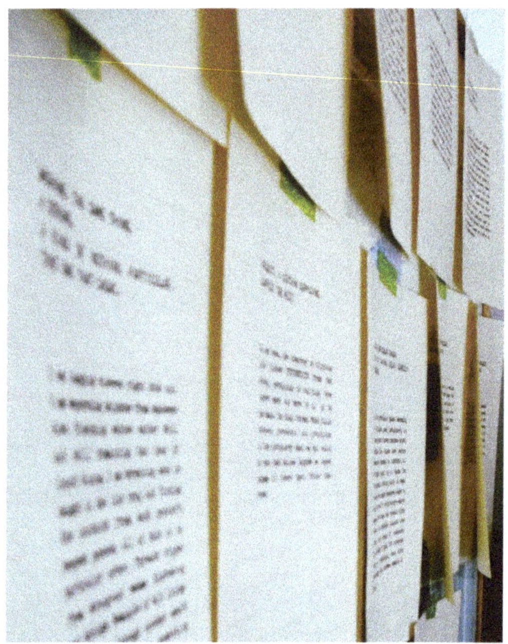

I'd been in the habit of tacking poems-in-process to the wall of my writing space, a small nook in the corner of my bedroom, next to a south-facing window. Writing the poems that make up *Illusory Borders*, I was influenced by poets I was reading— Susan Howe, Mei-me-Berssenbrugge, C.D. Wright—poets whose writing employs collage, whether seen or unseen, as an element in the poetic process. I recall it was Wright's *Deepstep Come Shining* that inspired me to combine my text on the wall (in this case, text defined as written or printed work) with images—primarily my growing collection of cyanotype prints.

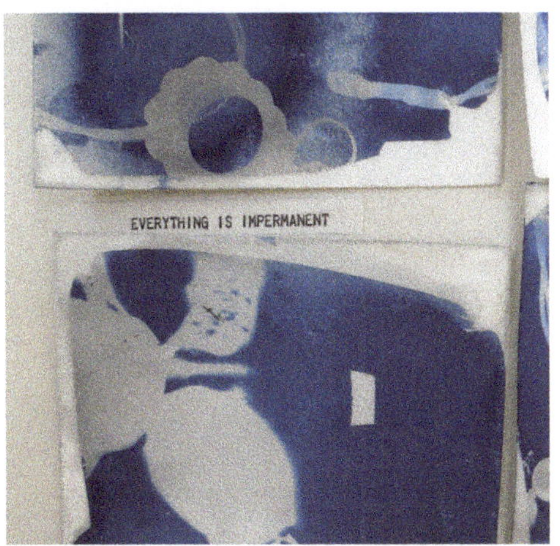

Wright's collection incorporates fragments of images, voices, memories, and folklore to create a lyrical collage or quilt, a text both dreamlike and cohesive. I say collage/quilt because as I was reading this book I found myself wanting to see the poetry mapped out on the wall, to get a visual sense of exactly how the threads and lines interacted. What held it all together?

I wasn't surprised to find, in my research, that Wright saw this poem on the wall, too. In an interview with Paul Magee in *The American Poetry Review*, Wright explains that her book was written during a month-long residency at the Virginia Center for Creative Arts (an art colony near Lexington, VA). "I had a white wall on which to mount my poem. I stared at it every day, like the painters in the Center were doing. I worked on it in an expressly visual way."

Wright describes hanging the text on the wall in columns, making the columns talk to each other. In *Deepstep*, the voices and images in conversation are pieced together to create a multi-layered fabric. In an interview published in Pen America, Daniel Schoonebeck writes: "The result, to use one of C.D. Wright's own words, is a welter of voices and images that weave a crosshatch throughout her entire body of work."

Over the course of a year and a half, I'd assembled my manuscript alongside hundreds of cyanotype prints—these included a series of 'moons' that together resembled a sort of lunar calendar. These cyanotypes were photograms of layers of tissue paper in a glass petri dish. On a few sunny winter days, I experimented using snow instead of tissue.

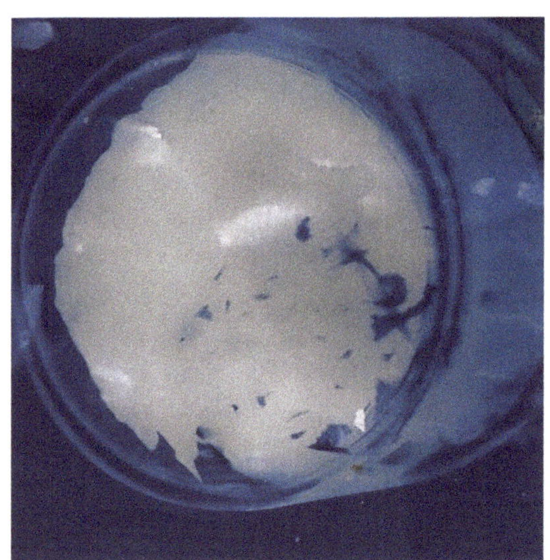

I stitched my accumulation of moons (literally, with a sewing machine) together with tanka poems (from a tanka diary I'd been keeping for several months) to create a patchwork of blue...

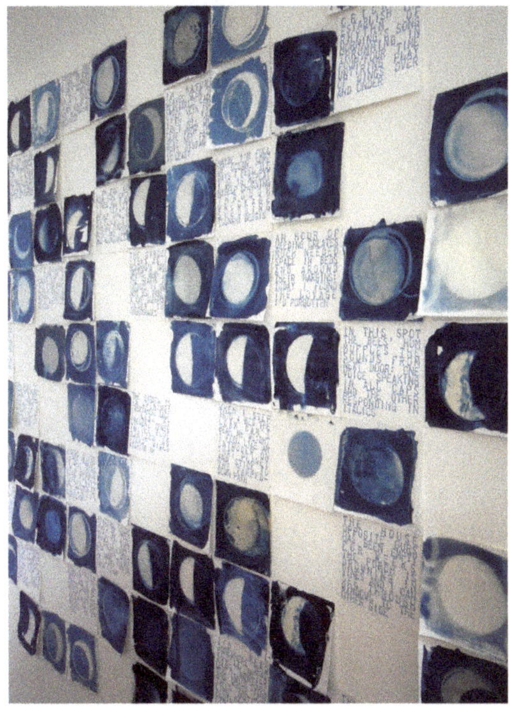

...and all of this eventually became a mixed media installation titled *Blue-ing*. Online, where these Field Notes live [on the OS's Medium page], you can see a short video clip of the installation in process at the Vermont College of Fine Arts in June 2015.

To some extent I think *Blue-ing*, as a text, exists separately from the series of poems that became *Illusory Borders*. But then I consider how *Blue-ing* documents/embodies my working through the process of writing...and the two become inseparable.

reference links:

https://aprweb.org/poems/an-interview-with-c-d-wright-by-paul-magee
https://pen.org/three-questions-with-c-d-wright/

FIELD NOTES Pt. 1-3 First Appeared online at The Operating System's platform on Medium—find process notes and documentation from Heidi Reszies and countless other creative practitioners in our long running FIELD NOTES series (and many other ongoing projects) at https://medium.com/the-operating-system/

OBJECTS AND THE SPACES THEY OCCUPY
A CONVERSATION WITH HEIDI RESZIES

Greetings! Thank you for talking to us about your process today!
Can you introduce yourself, in a way that you would choose?

Hello! My name is Heidi Reszies (pronounced REZ-zeez). I currently live in the city of Richmond, Virginia.

Why are you a poet/writer/artist?

I am at home/myself when I'm making things.

When did you decide you were a poet/writer/artist (and/or: do you feel comfortable calling yourself a poet/writer/artist, what other titles or affiliations do you prefer/feel are more accurate)?

I've considered myself an artist most of my life. I came to poetry/writing much later—during a traumatic shift, in my late 40s. I stopped painting and eventually turned to poetry as a way of healing. I don't think I actually thought of myself as a poet until my first poems were published; I remember introducing myself as a poet on the first day of my MFA Writing program at Vermont College of Fine Arts.

What's a "poet" (or "writer" or "artist") anyway? What do you see as your cultural and social role (in the literary / artistic / creative community and beyond)?

I like to think of poetry/writing/art under the umbrella of poiesis, derived from the ancient Greek, meaning 'to make.' Because I work across many disciplines in my creative practice, it's difficult to label myself/what I do. I usually choose transdisciplinary artist or maker.

I believe that human beings need poetry/art. Poetry saved my life. For me, poems exist in constellations, as potential/vital points of contact/connection/of being in the world.

Talk about the process or instinct to move these poems (or your work in general) as independent entities into a body of work. How and why did this happen? Have you had this intention for a while? What encouraged and/or confounded this (or a book, in general) coming together? Was it a struggle?

When I first began writing poems, I approached them as independent entities. At some point I discovered that the most natural way of making/writing, for me, is to work in series/sequence just as I had done in my years as a visual artist. When I set out to write this manuscript, I envisioned the text as a long poem/continuous stringing together of fragments.

Did you envision this collection as a collection or understand your process as writing or making specifically around a theme while the poems themselves were being written / the work was being made? How or how not?

I began writing the series of poems in the second section of the book, 'satellites & margins,' as a collection. The series titled 'preface(s)' was completed shortly after. I felt these two parts belonged together as a book. In terms of theme, I was writing/ making with attention to marginality, dailyness, and my necessity to work in a series.

What formal structures or other constrictive practices (if any) do you use in the creation of your work? Have certain teachers or instructive environments, or readings/writings/work of other creative people informed the way you work/write?

My creative practice negotiates text and textile; I typically begin with an accumulation of fragments of text, typed on a manual typewriter. I pin them to the wall or stitch them together (sometimes literally). I've found inspiration in the work of poets like Mei-mei Berssenbrugge, Susan Howe, Harryette Mullen, and Rosmarie Waldrop—poets who have described their creative processes as a sort of collage method—everyday objects assembled and arranged in a new composition. I'm grateful to Jody Gladding and Jen Bervin, two of my faculty advisors at VCFA, for their inspiration: for introducing me to 'gap gardening' and experimental ways of making poems.

Speaking of monikers, what does your title represent? How was it generated? Talk about the way you titled the book, and how your process of naming (individual pieces, sections, etc) influences you and/or colors your work specifically.

The title for this collection is in some ways a reflection on the in between, and my "tendency to linger at edges." I chose to name the two sections of this book, but individual poems are simply numbered (in the second section, footnotes are numbered), so as not to interrupt the nature of the series/sequence in which they were written. The section 'preface(s)' is... just that. The title 'satellites and margins' refers to book terminology, but also to the notion of fragments/objects and the spaces we/they occupy.

What does this particular work represent to you as indicative of your method/creative practice? your history? your mission/intentions/hopes/plans?

All I know is that these are poems that I had to write, one after the other, beginning again and again. And I continue to make poems in this way.

What does this book DO (as much as what it says or contains)?

This book cycles through a natural process...to borrow Allison Titus' words: "burgeoning and brimming and collapsing."

What would be the best possible outcome for this book? What might it do in the world, and how will its presence as an object facilitate your creative role in your community and beyond? What are your hopes for this book, and for your practice?

Once it's launched into the universe, I hope this book resonates with my readers / that it breathes / that it inspires.

Let's talk a little bit about the role of poetics and creative community in social and political activism, so present in our daily lives as we face the often sobering, sometimes dangerous realities of the Capitalocene. How does your process, practice, or work otherwise interface with these conditions?

Words matter. Language is not something we own; it is something we share.

I'd be curious to hear some of your thoughts on the challenges we face in speaking and publishing across lines of race, age, ability, class, privilege, social/cultural background, gender, sexuality (and other identifiers) within the community as well as creating and maintaining safe spaces, vs. the dangers of remaining and producing in isolated "silos" and/ or disciplinary and/or institutional bounds?

We should be striving for inclusivity in publishing. I appreciate what Audre Lourde writes (in *Age, Race, Class and Sex: Women Redefining Difference*):

"…it is not those differences between us that are separating us. It is rather our refusal to recognize those differences, and to examine the distortions which result from our misnaming them and their effects upon human behavior and expectation."

WHY PRINT DOCUMENT?

*The Operating System uses the language "print document" to differentiate from the book-object as part of our mission to distinguish the act of documentation-in-book-FORM from the act of publishing as a backwards-facing replication of the book's agentive *role* as it may have appeared the last several centuries of its history. Ultimately, I approach the book as TECHNOLOGY: one of a variety of printed documents (in this case, bound) that humans have invented and in turn used to archive and disseminate ideas, beliefs, stories, and other evidence of production.*

Ownership and use of printing presses and access to (or restriction of printed materials) has long been a site of struggle, related in many ways to revolutionary activity and the fight for civil rights and free speech all over the world. While (in many countries) the contemporary quotidian landscape has indeed drastically shifted in its access to platforms for sharing information and in the widespread ability to "publish" digitally, even with extremely limited resources, the importance of publication on physical media has not diminished. In fact, this may be the most critical time in recent history for activist groups, artists, and others to insist upon learning, establishing, and encouraging personal and community documentation practices. Hear me out.

With The OS's print endeavors I wanted to open up a conversation about this: the ultimately radical, transgressive act of creating PRINT /DOCUMENTATION in the digital age. It's a question of the archive, and of history: who gets to tell the story, and what evidence of our life, our behaviors, our experiences are we leaving behind? We can know little to nothing about the future into which we're leaving an unprecedentedly digital document trail — but we can be assured that publications, government agencies, museums, schools, and other institutional powers that be will continue to leave BOTH a digital and print version of their production for the official record. Will we?

As a (rogue) anthropologist and long time academic, I can easily pull up many accounts about how lives, behaviors, experiences — how THE STORY of a time or place — was pieced together using the deep study of correspondence, notebooks, and other physical documents which are no longer the norm in many lives and practices. As we move our creative behaviors towards digital note taking, and even audio and video, what can we predict about future technology that is in any way assuring that our stories will be accurately told – or told at all? How will we leave these things for the record?

In these documents we say: WE WERE HERE, WE EXISTED, WE HAVE A DIFFERENT STORY

- Lynne DeSilva-Johnson, Founder/Managing Editor,
THE OPERATING SYSTEM, Brooklyn NY 2019

RECENT & FORTHCOMING FULL LENGTH
OS PRINT::DOCUMENTS and PROJECTS, 2019-20

2019

Y - Lori Anderson Moseman
Ark Hive-Marthe Reed
I Made for You a New Machine and All it Does is Hope - Richard Lucyshyn
Illusory Borders-Heidi Reszies
A Year of Misreading the Wildcats - Orchid Tierney
Collaborative Precarity Bodyhacking Work-book and Research Guide - stormy budwig, Elae [Lynne DeSilva-Johnson] and Cory Tamler
We Are Never The Victims - Timothy DuWhite
Of Color: Poets' Ways of Making | An Anthology of Essays on Transformative Poetics -Amanda Galvan Huynh & Luisa A. Igloria, Editors
The Suitcase Tree - Filip Marinovich
In Corpore Sano: Creative Practice and the Challenged* Body - Elae [Lynne DeSilva-Johnson] and Amanda Glassman, Editors

KIN(D)* TEXTS AND PROJECTS

A Bony Framework for the Tangible Universe-D. Allen
Opera on TV-James Lowell Brunton
Hall of Waters-Berry Grass
Transitional Object-Adrian Silbernagel

GLOSSARIUM: UNSILENCED TEXTS AND TRANSLATIONS

Śnienie / Dreaming - Marta Zelwan, (Poland, trans. Victoria Miluch)
High Tide Of The Eyes - Bijan Elahi (Farsi-English/dual-language) trans. Rebecca Ruth Gould and Kayvan Tahmasebian
In the Drying Shed of Souls: Poetry from Cuba's Generation Zero Katherine Hedeen and Víctor Rodríguez Núñez, translators/editors

Street Gloss - Brent Armendinger with translations for Alejandro Méndez, Mercedes Roffé, Fabián Casas, Diana Bellessi, and Néstor Perlongher (Argentina)
Operation on a Malignant Body - Sergio Loo (Mexico, trans. Will Stockton)
Are There Copper Pipes in Heaven - Katrin Ottarsdóttir
(Faroe Islands, trans. Matthew Landrum)

2020

Institution is a Verb: a Panoply Performance Lab Compendium
— Esther Neff (PPL founder), Ayana Evans, Tsedaye Makonnen, Elizabeth Lamb, eds.
Acid Western — Robert Balun
Goodbye Wolf — Nik De Dominic
Cupping — Joseph Han
Poetry Machines: Letters for a Near Future — Margaret Rhee

KIN(D)* TEXTS AND PROJECTS

HOAX — Joey de Jesus
RoseSunWater — Angel Dominguez
Intergalactic Travels: poems from a Fugitive Alien — Alan Pelaez Lopez
Survivor— Joanna C. Valente

GLOSSARIUM: UNSILENCED TEXTS AND TRANSLATIONS

en el entre / in the between : Selected Antena Writings—Antena Aire (Jen Hofer & John Pluecker)
Híkurí [Peyote] — José Vincente Anaya (tr. Joshua Pollock)
Si la Musique Doit Mourir [If Music Were To Die] — Tahar Bekri (tr. Amira Rammah)
Zugunruhe — Kelly Martínez-Grandal (tr. Margaret Randall)
Black and Blue Partition ('Mistry) — Monchoachi (tr. Patricia Hartland)
Farvernes Metafysik: Kosmisk FarvelæreThe Metaphysics of Color: A Cosmic Theory of Color]
— Ole Jensen Nyrén (tr. Careen Shannon)

DOC U MENT
/däkyəmənt/

First meant "instruction" or "evidence," whether written or not.

noun - a piece of written, printed, or electronic matter that provides information or evidence or that serves as an official record
verb - record (something) in written, photographic, or other form
synonyms - paper - deed - record - writing - act - instrument

[*Middle English, precept, from Old French, from Latin documentum, example, proof, from docre, to teach; see dek- in Indo-European roots.*]

Who is responsible for the manufacture of value?

Based on what supercilious ontology have we landed in a space where we vie against other creative people
in vain pursuit of the fleeting credibilities of the scarcity economy, rather than
freely collaborating and sharing openly with each other in ecstatic celebration of MAKING?

While we understand and acknowledge the economic pressures and fear-mongering that threatens to
dominate and crush the creative impulse, we also believe that ***now more than ever we have the tools to
relinquish agency via cooperative means,*** fueled by the fires of the Open Source Movement.

**Looking out across the invisible vistas of that rhizomatic parallel country we can begin to see our
community beyond constraints, in the place where intention meets
resilient, proactive, collaborative organization.**

Here is a document born of that belief, sown purely of imagination and will.
When we document we assert. We print to make real, to reify our being there.
When we do so with mindful intention to address our process, to open our work to others,
to create beauty in words in space, to respect and acknowledge the strength of the page we now hold
physical, a thing in our hand… we remind ourselves that, like Dorothy: *we had the power all along, my dears.*

THE PRINT! DOCUMENT SERIES

is a project of
the trouble with bartleby
in collaboration with
the operating system

www.ingramcontent.com/pod-product-compliance
Lightning Source LLC
Chambersburg PA
CBHW042048030726
47599CB00019B/2407